The Philosopher's Club

Poems

by

Kim Addonizio

Foreword by Gerald Stern

BOA EDITIONS, LTD • ROCHESTER, NY

LC #: 93–74021

ISBN: 1–880238–03–9 Paper

99 00 01 02 7 6 5 4 3

The publication of books by BOA Editions, Ltd.,
is made possible with the assistance of grants from
the Literature Program of the New York State Council on the Arts
and the Literature Program of the National Endowment for the Arts,
as well as from the Lannan Foundation, and the Lila Wallace – Reader's
Digest Literary Publishers Marketing Development Program.

Cover Design: Daphne Poulin
Typesetting: Foerster FineLines, York Beach, ME
Manufacturing: McNaughton & Gunn, Lithographers
BOA Logo: Mirko

BOA Editions, Ltd.
Richard Garth, Chair
A. Poulin, Jr., Founder and President (1976-1996)
260 East Ave.,
Rochester, NY 14604

for you, Mom
and
for Aya

Their spirits haunt our minds, ears pressed to the
bones of our foreheads. Who can say how intently
they listen as we speak, or for what word?
        Gene Wolfe, The Citadel of the Autarch

Or discendiam qua giù nel cieco mondo.
        Dante, Inferno, *Canto IV*

Contents

3 Real Life

Foreword

There are some poets who write with a kind of foreknowledge—I'll call it that—and it is what gives these poets their strange power. It's as if life has already happened—as it happens—and they give in knowingly, even as they still struggle with desire and hope. Kim Addonizio is one of these. She is one who *knows*, somehow, and this knowledge itself gives strength and pity and tenderness, sometimes even terror, to her poems.

"The Philosopher's Club," the title poem of this remarkable first book of poems, is a good example. She remembers, with grief and joy, the meeting every week of a group of young students at a bar "around the corner from the streetcar tracks / at the West Portal Tunnel," where they drank "shooters" and talked for hours—after class—about sex and pregnancy and rape and murder before they hugged each other good night in front of "a lit streetcar," preparing to enter the tunnel, all this presided over by a bored bartender who stares angrily at the students and flips channels. Or "In Late Summer" where "*Sotto voce,* a woman croons / under the water"; or "His Ghost, Again" where her father returns to watch her dance and "cuts in / and leads me outside, makes me look at the sky."

In these poems, there is an unabashed willingness to let memory enter and take over; they are purgatorial, and elegiac, and unashamed. They touch the borders, of course; such poems insist on touching borders, and they flirt with self-love and spidery self-contemplation the way a reckless person flirts with deep water or with the metal plates at the edge of a bridge, but they save themselves from falling—and from drowning—through their accuracy, their precision, and their desperate search for understanding.

I think it's the voice of the poem that saves this author from drowning. I am moved by this voice. It's absolutely open, direct, loving, kind, a little sultry sometimes, marvelously self-knowing. And it's a voice that uses very little chicanery, and no subterfuge. Though decently subversive, and iconoclastic. The instrument is the cello, the voice is alto, the organ is the one inside the ribs.

And I love the erotic poems; they are of the best I have read in years. There is no double message, no politics. Sexual pleasure is in itself a good, nor is it recollected quite in tranquility. One poem reconstructs, with the added advantage, the added pleasure, of a mind alone remembering adolescent summer evenings, how beaus sat on "high / lifeguard chairs, eyes hidden by shades, / or came up behind us to grab the fat we hated / around our waists"; and another remembers the speaker walking naked and dripping after a bath out onto the porch and surprising two fawns resting in the grass, and being surprised by them.

> We have surprised each other;
> their soft black noses
>
> swing away from my breasts,
> quivering.

The fawns' noses and her breasts merge with each other. The "quivering" belongs to them both, though obviously the key word here is "swing." In the second part of the poem the lover, like a deer, is "nuzzling" the beloved, and the poem exquisitely confounds the "deer" experience with the sexual one.

> I remember you nuzzling me,
> raising my hips,
>
> my cheek against the mattress buttons.
> The little deer
>
> have been at the berries,
> nibbling stems. The doe eases out
>
> from the bushes,
> juice streaking her flanks.
>
> They follow her away down the hill
> and the wet

flattened grass
slowly rises behind them.

The erotic is always tender. There is no assault or invasion, no ugly secrets or dark shadows. That is, the erotic *is* love poetry, and when the issue in a poem is love as such, the tone is the same as it was in a more sexual poem. In a poem titled "Words Written During Your Operation," she says, "It's possible you won't wake; / I've no faith in anyone / who doesn't love you"; and in a superb poem called "Visit," she makes love to her lover in his dying mother's bed, yet there is nothing grotesque or disquieting about it.

These are lovely poems. Some are in open form and some—especially the remarkable group of sonnets in the second section—are quite strict. They represent a significant achievement and have in them the promise of more, of additional, fine work. I congratulate her.

— *Gerald Stern*

1
Heaven

What the Dead Fear

On winter nights, the dead
see their photographs slipped
from the windows of wallets,
their letters stuffed in a box
with the clothes for Goodwill.
No one remembers their jokes,
their nervous habits, their dread
of enclosed places.
In these nightmares, the dead feel
the soft nub of the eraser
lightening their bones. They wake up
in a panic, go for a glass of milk
and see the moon, the fresh snow,
the stripped trees.
Maybe they fix a turkey sandwich,
or watch the patterns on the TV.
It's all a dream anyway.
In a few months
they'll turn the clocks ahead,
and when they sleep they'll know the living
are grieving for them, unbearably lonely
and indifferent to beauty. On these nights
the dead feel better. They rise
in the morning, refreshed, and when the cut
flowers are laid before their names
they smile like shy brides. Thank you,
thank you, they say. You shouldn't have,
they say, but very softly, so it sounds
like the wind, like nothing human.

China Camp, California

Here's the long trough, covered by a screen,
where they cleaned shrimp.
Easier to imagine their catch
than to glimpse the ghosts of the fishermen
who lived here in these few wood buildings,
some now in need of repair, tin-roofed,
boarded windows whose gaps we peer through
to see shadowed dirt, a rusted wheelbarrow.
Of their boats, only a lone hull remains,
hauled to the sand and half-sunk there,
surrounded by chain link.
Yet everything is the same: the bay,
tamed by the curve of land that makes the cove,
still curls in
easily as hands turning over
to close, and close again, a book whose pages
ceaselessly open. Shards of their dishes
and rice bowls wash back
with the frail skeletons of crabs, glass
dulled and polished, indecipherable bits
of broken shells, jade-green kelp.
It's said they were driven out by hatred,
or concern that they'd leave nothing
for the next boats, but no one recorded
where they went. This was the home they made,
miles from China: brief shore,
a sky brushed with clouds,
gulls following them in each sunset,
the women stirring soup
with buried spoons, lost silk
of their sashes, black hair unpinned
and carried out with the tide,
tangling in the empty nets and sinking
to the coldest dark water.

The Concept of God

Years later, nothing inside the church
has changed. Not the dusty light,
not the white feet of the statues
or the boys in their pale smocks
kneeling before the candles.
Not the cool basement, the paper plates of donuts
set out by the coffee urns.
Not the bathroom with its stall doors open
on a row of immaculate toilets,
blue water in the bowls,
a small wrapped soap on each sink.
Forever the two girls leaning against the wall
in the deep quiet, sharing a lipsticked Salem
and watching themselves in the mirror,
forever the priest nodding in the confessional,
closing and opening and closing his small window.
Always my father moving down the rows
of bored, sonorous voices, passing the long-handled basket,
my mother with his handkerchief pinned over her hair.
Always, too, his coffin before the altar, my brother
stammering a eulogy, the long line of parked cars
spattered with snow. Always this brief moment
when the candles shudder, then resume,
and the girl holding the cigarette peers more closely
into the mirror, startled for an instant
at how old, how much like a woman
it makes her look.

Suffering: A Game

Let's imagine an ordinary man —
untouched by atrocities, indifferent
to the world, which he considers to exist
someplace beyond the roof of his neighbor's house,
the last on the cul-de-sac, beyond
the soapy scent of his wife as she sinks
into bed beside him and companionably
turns away, snoring lightly, her hair loose
over his left arm. Let's lift
him from her and shove him into line
behind those others, the survivors
of the camps who live long enough
to tell their story before dying of it,
or the ones whose names aren't recorded
anywhere, not even scratched into the bare
dirt with a bald stick, let's set him down
next to the ones he's been separated from
by accident, by history, by things
we can't control. Let's say he's different
from them — you can see he's definitely fatter,
slower and probably stupider — and his face,
with no grief to give it character,
is oddly shapeless, though now
you notice he's nervously looking around
for his wife and calling her name,
while all around him the others
press closer, reaching out their hands to him.
This is where the game always ends, because now
he's almost like them; I can't help feeling sorry
for the poor bastard, and so I let him go.
I let him run across his own yard,
throw the bolt and hurl himself beneath
the covers with his sleeping wife.
She's dreaming something awful she won't
remember, except for the lingering sense

of dread she'll feel on waking. Let's leave them
alone, they are the spared; draw the darkening sky
over them, tuck each flickering star
into its enviable, incriminating silence.

Event

The small arena almost filled,
the vendors pulling foamy beer
from rows of taps,

around the ring the long tables
of judges and sportswriters,
the bald promoter,

a photographer leaning in,
one elbow on the canvas to catch
a glove at the precise moment

it connects, the microphones carrying
the smack of leather up through wires,
satellites, into living rooms

though the spectators in the back
can't hear it,
or the man in the twelfth row listening

to the three behind him, cursing
the fighter this man has money on —
Nigger, pussy, fucking bum —

until the man turns around with
Shut the fuck up
and grabs one by the hair,

the two struggling briefly
as the crowd absorbs them
and settles them down.

Now the two knocks announcing ten seconds
to the end of the round; they stagger
to separate corners for comfort

and advice, icy water poured
down the silk shorts of one, chilled
metal held to the other's blossoming eye,

his good one following the ring girl
climbing in, holding aloft the time left
as she circles in her dangerous spiked heels

and white strip of bathing suit
to whistles and applause.
If you're waiting for more than this —

the names of the fighters, say,
or the outcome of the match, a decision
no one will agree with,

that will enter the record
of losses and temporary victories,
of the body's weight each struggles to maintain,

if you're waiting for the girl
to lie down under you
and moan your own name

in some damp corner of your dreams,
then you know why you're here
and why I can't tell you anything.

You know why you're aching
and have to keep taking it,
you recognize that roaring in your ears.

Full Moon

All over the city
something gets into people.
Women tucking in their kids
close their eyes, think of men
they should have followed off buses.
Girls rouge their cheeks with lipstick,
their bodies telling lies
to anyone who'll listen.
Cars with their lights off glide
under the trees, headed for the ocean.
The men going through garbage cans
rifle Burger King bags for a few
pale fries. They lie down
in doorways. In dreams, their mothers
check their foreheads for fever.
Refugees sit up
studying old photographs they enter
like water, going under.
Moon, take them down.
Desire is a cold drink
that scalds the heart.
Somewhere women are standing
at their windows, like lit candles,
and boys in Army boots
go dancing through the streets,
singing, and shoot
at anything that moves.

In Late Summer

Twilight: the last ferry leaves Vancouver
for the tiny islands.
Tsawassin blinks out,
rows of bolted plastic chairs
and old vending machines
gone blurred, crossing over.
Sotto voce, a woman croons
under the water, her hair
spilling luminous and phosphorescent
across the depths. The drowned
love this hour, before the stars
are let down like bait to tempt them,
before the steam moans out
and the captain settles back for a smoke.
The others on the boat
talk, drink coffee, drift upstairs;
two lovers stand at the railing
for the sheer terror of feeling
something might happen.
A moment ago they were sure
they would die for each other.
Then the kiss ended —
she leaned a little away,
his arm fell, everyone
turned towards the islands
they knew were out there,
willing them to appear.

Summer in the City

after Edward Hopper

When he finished with her and the afternoon,
he turned his face to the sheets.
She sat on the edge of the bed,
her breasts released from his hands
that had squeezed her too tightly
like the bra's elastic she'd unsnapped
when he asked her. She was tired
of saying no, those slow days waiting
on tables, taking the plates of eggs
from his fingers, seeing how he watched her
while the meat sputtered on the grill
in its murky fat, taking his eyes
until she felt him inside her
as she moved down the counter pouring coffee.
Now he lies there dreaming,
but not of her, and she
has stepped into the red dress and pulled it
almost to her breasts before sitting back down.
She can't decide if she should stay
or leave, walk out into the dark
the light comes from and put on her uniform
for the late customers.
She knows those faces,
how they'll open like a row of flowers,
drinking what she gives them. The man
will come in later,
tying on a fresh apron and avoiding her eyes,
his hands clean, smelling of soap and cigarettes.

Explication

Waiting behind barbed wire
are the people about to be
ashes, then smoke

billowing over the Czech countryside.
In the film, the camera briefly pans
the mothers, children, a few old men

leaning on their crutches,
then abandons them to history.
Watching this scene

we feel only a momentary horror
because Kominek is the one
we are watching, Kominek

dancing a little as he passes them
because he has bread.
The Slovak has been spared

because the Commandant needs
a sparring partner, someone
who can stand up to him

in a makeshift ring;
every three days
they fight again, and each time

the prisoner gets a little stronger,
until at last he knows he can
beat him, can drive his gloved fist

hard into the harsh face
and make it yield. And because this
is what we hope for,

from the first barrage of blows
the Commandant inflicts
on the starving prisoner

before he starts to fatten him,
and because Kominek looks so happy
passing the restless mass behind

the fence, the kids
crying a little, we can almost
ignore them, as he does

on his way back to the barracks —
and the camera lets us,
for a while, until

it returns, to move slowly over
what they've left behind.
Crutches lying in mud,

carriage on its side,
fringed shawl,
black-haired doll against the fence —

these mute objects
bear witness to a moment
we looked away,

or didn't look hard enough,
while at the margins
of our attention men

and children,
women, a whole world
disappeared,

rose and floated off
in a light breeze,
smoke above the arms of trees.

The Call

A man opens a magazine,
women with no clothes,
their eyes blacked out.
He dials a number,
hums a commercial
under his breath. A voice
tells him he can do
anything he wants to her.
He imagines standing her
against a wall, her saying
Oh baby you feel so good.
It's late. The woman
on the phone yawns,
trails the cord to the hall
to look in on her daughter.
She's curled with one
leg off the couch.
The woman shoulders the receiver,
tucks a sheet and whispers
Yes, do it, yes.
She drifts to the kitchen,
opens another Diet Pepsi, wonders
how long it will take him and where
she can find a cheap winter coat.
Remembering the bills,
she flips off the light.
He's still saying *Soon,*
turning his wheelchair right,
left, right. A tube runs down
his pants leg. Sometimes
he thinks he feels something,
stops talking to concentrate
on movement down there.
Hello, the woman says.
You still on?

She rubs a hand over her eyes.
Blue shadow comes off on her fingers.
Over the faint high hiss
of the open line
she hears the wheels knock
from table to wall.
What's that, she says.
Nothing, he tells her,
and they both
listen to it.

The Philosopher's Club

After class Thursday nights
the students meet at the Philosopher's Club.
It's right around the corner from the streetcar tracks
at the West Portal tunnel. No one bothers
to check I.D.s. Five or six of them
get shooters and talk — about sex, usually.
Let me tell you about this dildo I bought,
one girl says. She describes how it looks
when all the gadgets attached to it are going at once.
My girlfriend is pregnant, says one of the boys.
That's nothing, says another, I've got twins
I've never seen. It goes on like this all semester.
Gradually they learn each other's stories:
the girl raped at knifepoint in Florida,
the kid whose old man shot seven people
in a trailer park outside Detroit.
Life is weird, they agree, touching glasses.
The bartender flips channels on the TV,
the sound turned down.
Spoiled brats, he thinks. He imagines a woman
with the blonde's legs, the brunette's tits.
"Dynasty" looks boring and he quits
at a black-and-white newsreel about the Nazi camps —
piles of heads with their mouths open,
bodies with arms like chicken wings. On the jukebox
Otis Redding sings "Try a Little Tenderness."
One of the regulars stands there
popping his gum, jamming in selections.
The students, smashed, are hugging each other.
I love you, they all say. Outside, in the rain,
people are boarding a lit streetcar.
As it jolts towards the tunnel
some of them look back at the bar,
its staticky neon sign
the last thing they see as they enter the dark.

Heaven

Under the yellow tent, the dead drink
zombies, make small talk and slap at mosquitoes.
Death is no different from life when it comes
to stupid parties.
The band's bad singer edges
into the high notes, the smoked salmon
is squashed under someone's briefcase.
A drunk woman in a green dress proposes
to a man she just met. The guest of honor
has disappeared, not that anyone notices.
Dead people disappear all the time.

The bar is out of limes again.
A dead American sits on a trash can, talking
to a Salvadoran, listening to his tales of torture.
That's tough, the American says; I died instantly,
in a car wreck, after one too many
at the Tic Toc Lounge. See that woman
with the red hair? She was with me.
She won't speak to me unless I quit drinking.
Why quit now? The American laughs,
falls off the trash can.
The Salvadoran helps him up,
thinks of his prison cell, the jokes
his torturers told. Why remember all that? he thinks.
He watches a woman in a sari, dancing alone.
She died in childbirth, of a fever. Her baby starved
a few days later. Right now he's lying
in a playpen by the piano, gumming a rubber lamb.
I could dance with her, the Salvadoran tells himself,
but he doesn't move.

In the dark by the rose garden
two people are arguing.
The woman leans her forehead against a tree.
She picks at the bark, wanting to hit something.
The man wants to hit her, but when he grabs her
she cries in his arms. What a party this is.
Open-air, anyone can come,
people drift in and out at all hours.
If only we could have some privacy, the woman sobs.
Just then a retired grocer who was blown up

along with a few dozen people
drops down beside them. Where am I? he says.
The couple stares at him and he wanders off
toward the lights of the tent.
He thinks he's in heaven, seeing the bar,
the beautiful women, the baby drooling and smiling.
Is this heaven? he asks the sax player,
between sets. No answer. Shrugging, he goes off
into the bushes to piss. When he turns back,
the tent, the people, the lousy band
have all disappeared.
Only the couple is still there.
He walks over, punches the man
and watches him fall into nothingness.
He drags the woman into the grass and rapes her,
but just as he's about to come she vanishes.
He's left holding himself. Alone at last.
What now? he thinks. He turns over
on his back and stares at the sky, the lights
of all those long-dead stars
going out one by one.

Sestina of the Alcoholic Daughter

I keep returning to that muttering woman
huddled at a table by the window,
one arm bandaged, the bandages old
and filthy, her scabbed hands
curled around a coffee cup. That was late afternoon,
the donut shop; it's night now, and I'm home:

cat, fried eggs, blue robe, Beefeaters — home
to me at least, although a woman
like my mother, whom I saw this afternoon
for lunch, might say *Look at you,* make a window
of thumbs and forefingers and hold out her hands
accusingly, telling me I'm too old

to still live alone, and old
enough to know two rooms aren't a home.
I think of my mother's shaking hands
raising a spoon, or smoothing her hospital gown, this woman
who forgets my name, and hers, who stared out the window
and made incoherent conversation all afternoon.

If it were still this afternoon,
I might answer her now: old
mother, madwoman, widow, who is it that window
reflects? It's this nursing home
that's lacking, where a bitter, crazy woman
sings of the past and wrings her hands.

Of our two lonelinesses, mother, yours wins. Hands
down, your dim stale room in the long afternoon
is a worse nightmare. But I'm drunk now; and a drunk woman
is a pathetic thing, isn't she — any old
misery, any discomfort, will suffice to bring home
the knowledge that I'd just as soon leap from the window

as face my own life in the mirror. And the window
is a mirror, these hours I sit with my hands
clenched in my lap, looking out towards the Catholic Home
I left in anger just this afternoon,
knowing it's too late. You're too old,
no longer my mother but a strange woman

distant as that woman in the donut shop window, oblivious
of the afternoon. For an old instant, mother, I wanted to take
her hands in mine — to lead her home, trusting we'd find the way.

Pantoum: At Mount Hebron

for Zelman

This cemetery is no haven,
old Jews waving at you
offering Kaddish for a few dollars,
cars crowding the two roads through —

Old Jews waving at you
beginning their prayers, bowing and bowing,
cars crowding the two roads through
and you walk along the rows. All the sons

beginning their prayers, bowing and bowing.
You stand before your father
and you walk along the rows
going on and on.

You stand before your father
where you stood all your life
going on and on
with words he can't hear.

Where you stood all your life
was the same place: offering your love
with words he couldn't hear.
This cemetery is no haven.

His Ghost, Again

I'm tired of my father coming around.
He sits in a wing chair
in the oak-paneled room,
watching me dance with a man
while another man plays the piano.
The man holds me hard against him.
I think of pressing on a wound
to stop the blood. He breathes
sweat from my skin.
I see morning,
my body arcing into his hand,
my dress on the floor by his bed.
My father cuts in
and leads me outside,
makes me look at the sky.
They're up there, he says.
You can't imagine their brightness.
I move out from under
his arm on my shoulder.
Behind us, a dark bottle
on the piano cover, an apple,
fingers finding the sweetest low notes.

Ange de Morte

Christian Boltanski, "Lessons of Darkness,"
University Art Museum, Berkeley

These two
tiny figures, suspended
by thin wires from the center
of the ceiling, circle continuously
in their separate orbits. In the darkened room
the projector blazes down, translating them into huge
winged shadows on the walls, each angel traveling towards
the other and passing through. This is how the world divides,
halving itself, until we turn and return to the brief confusion
of sex, working our shadows into other bodies, but feeling
them always drift back over us, settling like fine silt.
Walking out of the museum to the grey afternoon,
where it is raining steadily, you can sense
the big stone building at your back,
the room you will one day enter,
where the hands of the angels
will haul you up through
the black floor of the
sky, into your own
waiting arms.

The Last Poem About the Dead

sounds like this: a long sweet silence
the next soul breaks as it drops,
the way a fish flops back
slapping the quiet water,
the next slippery, gleaming body
that's still, this minute, alive:
my mother, the brothers I love
but can't get close to,
or my daughter,
please God not my daughter,
not her made-up songs
as she moves her dolls from kitchen to bed
in the small house; take
anyone else, my lover with his warm sex
pressed against me,
brush him off of me like a winged insect,
I don't care what you do with him,
you can have all of them,
my family, my best friend,
take them, but not my girl.
And if it's me
then the silence doesn't stop
when I hit the water, thrashing,
it goes on unless you do it
for me, make the poem I'd make
drifting down to them
without voice; oh, tell me
how to tell you what it's like.

2
Falling Through the World

The Sound

Marc says the suffering that we don't see
still makes a sort of sound — a subtle, soft
noise, nothing like the cries or screams that we
might think of — more the slight scrape of a hat doffed
by a quiet man, ignored as he stands back
to let a lovely woman pass, her dress
just brushing his coat. Or else it's like a crack
in an old foundation, slowly widening, the stress
and slippage going on unnoticed by
the family upstairs, the daughter leaving
for a date, her mother's resigned sigh
when she sees her. It's like the heaving
of a stone into a lake, before it drops.
It's shy, it's barely there. It never stops.

On Opening a Book of Photographs

I look at them until I feel immune,
a pile of bodies photographed by Lee
Miller, nineteen forty-five, their strewn
limbs, at first random, now obviously
framed — four legs, like spokes, ray out
across the page. That checkered rag — a dress,
maybe, or only a piece of cloth — I doubt
it covers a woman. The others' sex
is easy: they're men; their faces, and
two exposed penises, nested in shadowed
groins, look tender, peaceful, like that hand
curled on a chest, as if it knows
where it rests. But it doesn't. However I
tell this, they're not redeemed. There they lie.

Aquarium

The fish are drifting calmly in their tank
between the green reeds, lit by a white glow
that passes for the sun. Blindly, the blank
glass that holds them in displays their slow
progress from end to end, familiar rocks
set into the gravel, murmuring rows
of filters, a universe the flying fox
and glass cats, Congo tetras, bristle-nosed
plecostemus all take for granted. Yet
the platys, gold and red, persist in leaping
occasionally, as if they can't quite let
alone a possibility — of wings,
maybe, once they reach the air? They die
on the rug. We find them there, eyes open in surprise.

Man on a Corner

The man with the golden retriever is still sitting
against the bank's brick wall on his blanket, while
all along the street the store owners are quitting,
a florist carrying in bouquets, the mild
fragrance of the flowers a brief antidote
to the exhaust of a bus, just releasing
its passengers; they swirl around him, like notes
of some random music, scattering in the increasing
dusk. Now the prone dog lifts its head
and looks at him, as though a sudden thought's
occurred to it; the man still slumps, dead
or dreaming, figure in a drama not
of the dog's making, but all it knows
of love; it shifts, sighs, lays its head close.

February 14, 1989

North's lawyers say he'll claim a cover-up.
In Pakistan, mobs riot, and police
open fire; everywhere in Europe
Gorbachov's perceived as wanting peace,
which has NATO worried. Kabul, in blue
cold, sees the last Red Army soldiers go,
with Najibulla's government the new
target for guerillas. By a row
of houses underneath a freeway, a man
watches the little girl he wants to lift
out of her life skip towards his waiting van.
The earth's not turning, love; it only shifts
direction in its falling through the world.
The roses you brought have opened.

First Poem for You

I like to touch your tattoos in complete
darkness, when I can't see them. I'm sure of
where they are, know by heart the neat
lines of lightning pulsing just above
your nipple, can find, as if by instinct, the blue
swirls of water on your shoulder where a serpent
twists, facing a dragon. When I pull you
to me, taking you until we're spent
and quiet on the sheets, I love to kiss
the pictures in your skin. They'll last until
you're seared to ashes; whatever persists
or turns to pain between us, they will still
be there. Such permanence is terrifying.
So I touch them in the dark; but touch them, trying.

Address

Lacking the intimate *tu,* and with *thou*
fallen out of fashion, I can only use
a neutral word, one that won't allow
me to explain how, as I lose
myself in that hour of the afternoon
when I feel most afraid, uncertain
of what's coming, knowing only that it's soon —
how as I lie down, drawing the curtains
like a patient in a hospital, I'm filled
with what the day's forgotten, all the stray
images, stories, the small acts of will
that won't matter, the sound of the bay
insistent, meaningless, without clues —
how I want to say it, what I most fear losing:

Solace

I found a nest this morning, in the grass
beside the road. I had run out to see
the train from Monroe, catching just the last
few cars disappearing through the trees.
Dried mud clung to the nest. Inside, nothing:
as I held it, tiny bugs swarmed up my hand.
I don't know what I wanted — something
more — an egg, or just a shell, some strand
of meaning. I wonder if my mother stood
over her mother's bed like this, on finding
she'd died during the night, wearing her good
nightgown — as if preparing, and not minding.
My mother must have waited for a sign, a sense
someone was near. I think she found only silence.

Lullaby

This hammock, slung between two trees, exists
so there might stumble to it, drunk, one night
with a blanket, three people the moon enlists
to remind itself it's lovely, like the white
back of a woman bathing as she kneels
at the edge of a river, lifting the shivering water
to her face in cupped hands. Which now is the real
tableau: this luminous, naked body, or
the three friends? Rocking quietly, their heads
close together, they are almost happy. Each
has separate sorrows, and in their separate beds
they'll feel this moment moving out of reach,
receding. But let's keep them touching here
a little longer, voices raised against the air.

3
Real Life

Them

That summer they had cars, soft roofs crumpling
over the back seats. Soft, too, the delicate fuzz
on their upper lips and the napes of their necks,
their uneven breath, their tongues tasting
of toothpaste. We stole the liquor
glowing in our parents' cabinets, poured it
over the cool cubes of ice with their hollows
at each end, as though a thumb had pressed
into them. The boys rose, dripping, from long
blue pools, the water slick on their backs
and bellies, a sugary glaze; they sat easily on high
lifeguard chairs, eyes hidden by shades,
or came up behind us to grab the fat we hated
around our waists. For us it was the chaos
of makeup on a bureau, the clothes we tried on
and on, the bras they unhooked, pushed
up, and when they moved their hard
hidden cocks against us we were always
princesses, our legs locked. By then we knew
they would come, climb the tower, slay anything
to get to us. We knew we had what they wanted:
the breasts, the thighs, the damp hairs pressed flat
under our panties. All they asked was that we let them
take it. They would draw it out of us like
sticky taffy, thinner and thinner until it snapped
and they had it. And we would grow up
with that lack, until we learned how to
name it, how to look in their eyes and see nothing
we had not given them; and we could still
have it, we could reach right down into their
bodies and steal it back.

The Night Princess

I discover your lace glove
under my pillow.
Your rings of pure glass
gleam on the bureau
with crayons and bracelets.
When I get up
late at night, I step
on animals whose fur
you clutched and released.
I am awake
in the freezing kitchen,
noticing how your easel
looms in one corner,
how your paintings disguise
the door to the porch.
These nights I feel
more ghost than mother,
adrift in the castle
you build day by day —
your life holding me in,
my own life diminishing
as my mother's diminished
to the size of the pea
in the fairy tale, hard
as a marble under the mattress,
the one you'll feel
years from now
as you struggle with sleep.

Reminder

There was a man in the bar tonight
turning his wheelchair in slow half-circles,
digging patterns into the sawdust
and talking about the whores on Tu Do Street
to various women, who seemed to feel obliged to listen,
paralyzed in attitudes of polite sympathy.
They clutched their drinks and nodded,
looking stricken, until he turned away abruptly
and stopped speaking.
Then he simply drained his beer and left.
It was the beginning of my shift, and as I worked
I thought of him, returning to a room
where he would lift his half-limp body into bed
and dream — not of the dead,
who probably seldom bothered with him now, but of the women.
I once loved a man like that,
though we've lost touch —
we used to spend nights together,
after his awkward bathroom ritual with the plastic gloves,
after the arrangement of the pillows
and the long tube from his penis.
I would take my clothes off for him
in the dimmed light, and then bite his nipples,
where he felt the most pleasure.
He'd talk of fucking me until it meant
something different — not the act itself,
which he had never experienced, but this
careful passion, his legs sprawled helplessly
over the sheets, my body moving slowly
against his hand. I wondered if the man in the bar
had someone, too, a woman stronger than I was,
able to stay with him
without the notion of sacrifice —
possibly he'd hoped to find her tonight,
her face softened by neon,

somewhere in the smoke and slam of the pool players.
I saw him turning and turning,
surveying the room of strangers.
Later I picked up his glass from the table;
the damp ring it left I wiped away;
that, at least, I could erase.

Alone in Your House

I walk naked and
dripping to the kitchen,

the floor sticky,
rubbing myself

with your damp towel.
When I go out on the porch

two fawns get up
from the grass.

We have surprised each other;
their soft black noses

swing away from my breasts,
quivering.

I remember you nuzzling me,
raising my hips,

my cheek against the mattress buttons.
The little deer

have been at the berries,
nibbling stems. The doe eases out

from the bushes,
juice streaking her flanks.

They follow her away down the hill
and the wet

flattened grass
slowly rises behind them.

Words Written During Your Operation

The early fog has retreated
to the highest hills, revealing
the nearer world: wood fence,
barn, clumped cows. Right now
the anaesthetist owns you
and has loaned you to the surgeon
with his scalpel and saw.
All flesh is meat; those slow forms
on the steep slope bow their heads
as if in grief, though they're innocent of it.
It's possible you won't wake;
I've no faith in anyone
who doesn't love you. How
can I trust even this blue,
that's arrived by stealth,
like a thief? Instead I hold on
to memory: you pursued me, you wouldn't
let me be; the idea
you'd leave me is beyond belief.

From Then to Now

for Dorianne

I've been thinking of your father,
who stood over your bed
and casually opened you,
who walked down the hall in his robe and slippers
after lifting the childhood from your body
night after night, the way the knife
lifts the delicate skeleton of the fish
from its flesh, the way the magician
slips the scarlet silk from his black sleeve.
I didn't know you then. At seven
I was picking out my birthday doll
in a hotel gift shop, and my father
was in that other world, the one where words
and gestures drifted idly down on
threads of smoke from his cigarettes
and the smell of his cologne. I felt alone
but I did not feel that terror
of my father's step. Whenever I
see you now, I see your father, too,
standing behind your shoulder in his pajamas,
a vague grey shape, oddly humble
in his refusal to vanish, his hands like two
hooks descending; and when we hug in greeting
it's him I take you from,
I put my arms around that sleepy child
and make him give her back.

One Day My Daughter Will Learn
About Anne Frank

She'll imagine snow falling,
Anne standing at the attic window

or writing in the book from Otto,
I asked Margot if she thought

I was very ugly.
She'll wonder

if she would have been taken from me,
would have watched the birds

in each camp scattering
across the frozen mud and then

lifting over the wires.
Maybe she'll lift her own eyes

to some God I never taught her to believe in,
though we lit the candles and blessed bread

and I touched the wine to her lips,
because she was still half a Jew,

still her father's daughter.
After learning about that other girl

my child will raise her small, troubled face
towards an idea of heaven

and feel all that snow,
its cold weight

bearing down until
she has to close her eyes,

the world will have turned
so terribly bright.

Cranes in August

They clutter the house,
awkwardly folded, unable
to rise. My daughter makes
and makes them, having heard
the old story: what we create
may save us. I string
a long line of them over
the window. Outside
the grey doves bring
their one vowel to the air,
the same sound
from many throats, repeated.

Real Life

Here we walk without wallets,
no keys to anything. The gates
swing open, we move among the
cows, hot hills, at night through wet
foxtails; the kitchen light hums,
winged things circle it. Yesterday
you slit a snakeskin and found
the diamond pattern interrupted,
in the center, by a heart:
covered it in salt, tacked
it to a board for drying out.
This evening it's soft, the scale
you peel for me a tiny
translucency in my hand.

Elephant Seals, Año Nuevo

There they lie, fasting and molting
and not moving, but for an occasional
stray flipper that idly rises
and sinks down, into the mass
of massive bodies.
This is their summer's work,
before the bulls swim in
to bloody each other for mates.
We watch their great sides heave,
the effort it takes to stay
where they've arrived, amazed
they've managed something we can't.
What would it be like
to live, slow and huge,
the low slopes of the dunes
marking a horizon whose limits
we weren't compelled to challenge?
For these seals there is no
path that leads away,
no car waiting
in the wavering heat of the parking lot,
and no road takes them
to the made world: here we're all
immensely complicated, and nothing,
my darling, is seasonal —
once you and I leave
this place, we won't return to it.

Visit

We lay in your mother's bed
which you had taken down off its casters,
next to her dresser with its hidden contents,
her bras and nylon underwear and slips
tangled together, the round fan on the sill
turning toward us like a drugged woman's face
and then slowly turning aside.
Your mother was lying in a hospital room,
we had her apartment to ourselves —
table pushed to the corner, magazines
sliding from a chair,
my suitcase spread open on the couch.
When we made love
we shoved the covers in a heap to the floor
and you pulled me over you
the way a nurse would one day pull the white sheet
over her, you lowered me onto your cock
the way a man would lower the satin-lined lid of the casket
until it clicked shut.
I lifted myself above you, moaning,
my breasts grazing your face,
the Christ on the wall was gazing down,
blood on His hands and feet
where they'd hammered the nails deep
into His flesh —
finally I collapsed against your chest
and felt you coming, shuddering,
letting your grief wash into me cell by cell.
As we lay there, breathing hard,
I listened to your heart gradually slowing
and when you wanted to rise I held you down,
with my smaller body
I kept you from danger a few minutes longer.

Late Round

When the fighters slow down, moving towards each other
as though underwater, gloves laboring to rise
before their faces, each punch followed by a clutch
when they hold on like exhausted lovers,
I think of us in the last months, and of the night
you stood in my kitchen, drunk, throwing wild combinations
at the air, at something between us that would not
go down. I watch the two of them
planted in that ring, unable to trust their legs,
the bell's reprieve suspended in some impossible distance,
and I remember my voice, cursing our life together
until there was nothing either one of us would fight for.
These men, you'd say, have heart — they keep on,
though neither remembers his strategy
or hears the shouts from his corner. And it's true
you had more heart than I did, until that night
you gave us up, finally, and dropped crying to your knees
on my kitchen floor. The fighters stagger and fall together,
flailing against the ropes. They embrace
and are separated, but they don't let go.

Conversation in Woodside

Joe insisted that life is extreme,
but Nadja and I argued for dailiness:
the stove's small flame under the kettle,
the lover who, turning over in bed,

reaches for an absence
that still holds your warmth, recoverable.
We were sitting after dinner, the wine finished,
our plates not yet cleared away,

and Joe, full of grief and memory,
said *My friends are dying every day.*
I thought of all the evidence
against us, against the pink poppies

opening in a glass vase, the fragrant candles,
the living room where the others were dancing
while we kept on, talking about loss,
and our childhoods, and whether evil

enters us from somewhere
or only lies dormant, waiting to bloom;
suddenly the dark outside the big windows,
rising from the fences and fields, seemed

to be listening, as though it needed
something from us, not permission exactly,
but something only we could give it.
And I felt we were safe, as long

as we stayed around the cluttered table,
safe, even, for the few days we'd spend working here,
and Joe tipped back on two legs
of his chair, balancing there.

Insomnia

How I envy the sleepers,
my neighbors. And you,
lying there with your arm
flung over your forehead

as if to keep me from waking you.
I wade into the chill of the hallway
where the black current runs,
old loves waiting for me

to slip beneath the water
and float drowned into their arms —
the body's surrender
almost better than the heart's.

I walk, shivering,
small fish sieving past.
They are traveling towards the one window
the grey light will fill,

dissolving them
almost to nothing,
vague intimations. But I switch on
the kitchen bulb,

and in that cold white silence
they collide, confused,
beginning their terrible transformation —
enormous now,

and with a hunger
that can't be eased
they cry out,
they flip their tails wildly,

they swerve towards me.

Gravity

Carrying my daughter to bed
I remember how light she once was,
no more than a husk in my arms.
There was a time I could not put her down,
so frantic was her crying if I tried
to pry her from me, so I held her
for hours at night, walking up and down the hall,
willing her to fall asleep. She'd grow quiet,
pressed against me, her small being alert
to each sound, the tension in my arms, she'd take
my nipple and gaze up at me,
blinking back fatigue she'd fight whatever terror
waited beyond my body in her dark crib. Now
that she's so heavy I stagger beneath her,
she slips easily from me, down
into her own dreaming. I stand over her bed,
fixed there like a second, dimmer star,
though the stars are not fixed: someone
once carried the weight of my life.

The Taste of Apples

All morning my daughter has been picking apples.
She brings them in a brown paper sack,
she is happy, she offers me one.
A while ago, thumbing through an early *Life* magazine,
I came across a photograph —
a solemn group of schoolchildren — and thought
of what time does, of how their faces
must have changed as the photographer finished
and they broke from their neat rows,
became men, women, old.
My oblivious child empties her sack
into my lap. . . . For the rest of the day
she plays quietly, moves them from room to room
with her dolls and animals, at last arranges them
in tender patterns on the rug.
Now, late at night, I want to write something
that can be offered, taken, eaten. If I say
window, sky, white apple, if I think of a black branch
bending but not breaking, will I have said
what I mean — that tonight, as I watched her
smoothing out a dress for morning, carefully,
before she turned her face up for a kiss, I knew
she had already gone from me, into her life.
Children in a photograph, the tart sweetness
of apples, my daughter's fingers
grimy with soil and smelling of her sex.
She mutters in her sleep. I keep a bowl
on the kitchen table, filled now with apples,
the hard, shiny fruits
I will bite into, one by one, savoring each.

Diorama: Maine

I cup my palm around the day
with its high clouds and breakers and the clean
wooden houses lining the shore. Cormorants
flying under the water, rising wet,
standing close together on the sharp rocks.
Men and women at a table, touching glasses,
and the clear sound carrying out for years.
We have come to Ogunquit
where the waiter is always arriving
and the lobsters still steam in their beds
of mussels, hard shells intact. Everything
has this edge: an outline like a child's
black crayon. The air sifts down to us
blue and salt-cold, and the world
is visible at last, and curves in
to this spit of land where we sit
as if anchored, tethered to each other
by the slenderest and brightest of ropes.

Potomac Photograph

That afternoon,
    just hours before your plane,
        we drove out River Road

so I could show you
    where they were buried,
        the acre of graves surrounded by houses,

neat lawns, a tennis court
    where someone was playing,
        the ball's monotonous *thunk*

drifting through the steel fence.
    In the cemetery
        I knelt and held my daughter;

over my shoulder
    she saw you raising your camera
        and waved you away.

But I wanted
    that picture of my grief;
        I wanted us there beside the graves

with the soda bottle of flowers she'd picked,
    to look at it later
        and know there was a moment

the dead and living were together.
    You understood that,
        knew that alone in your darkroom

we would float up to you,
    my face buried in her neck,
        hers small and sober,

the features sharpening.
       That stone over there is my grandmother,
           brushing and brushing her thin hair;

there's my father,
       sweating in his blue suit
           and those others crowding in

are strangers,
       who stroke the gold head
           of my child,

and that blur of bright
       continuous motion is her hand, waving,
           waving.

Beds

All night I turn between
lover and daughter, holding one
and then the other. Before dawn
I have slipped out of bed,
leaving them together,
the man's broad chest uncovered,
the child's blonde hair
hiding her face.
I remember nights as a child,
wedged between my parents,
the sinking down to sleep surrounded
by familiar things. When death
beats its wings at the window,
I hope I am not standing
alone in the kitchen
with a cup and a hairbrush,
watching doves on a wire.
I want to curl up
in that dim, disordered bed
where all my loves lie,
elbow to cheek;
I want the brief reprieve
as the angel who came for me
pauses, uncertain,
trying to distinguish one breath
from another.

Acknowledgments

Grateful acknowledgment is made to the editors of the following journals in which these poems first appeared:

Agni: "Explication"
Alchemy: "The Last Poem About the Dead"
Berkeley Poets Cooperative: "Alone in Your House"
Berkeley Poetry Review: "Ange de Morte"; "Beds"; "Full Moon"
Five Fingers Review: "The Night Princess"
Madison Review: "Sestina of the Alcoholic Daughter"
Mississippi Valley Review: "Heaven"; "On Opening a Book of Photographs"
MSS/New Myths: "Words Written During Your Operation"
New England Review: "The Concept of God"; "The Sound"; "The Taste of Apples"
Paris Review: "Pantoum: At Mount Hebron"
Poetry Flash: "What the Dead Fear"
Prairie Schooner: "China Camp, California"; "In Late Summer"; "Them"
Quarry West: "Summer in the City"
The Southern California Anthology: "Suffering: A Game"
The Sun: "Late Round"
Threepenny Review: "Conversation in Woodside"; "His Ghost, Again"; "The Philosopher's Club"

Some of these poems also appeared in the following anthologies: "Visit" in *Catholic Girls;* "Them" and "Reminder" in *Lovers;* "The Call" in *The Maverick Poets;* "The Philosopher's Club" in *A New Geography of Poets.* "Alone in Your House" and "The Call" were first published in *Three West Coast Women* (Five Fingers Poetry, 1987).

Thanks to the Corporation of Yaddo, the Djerassi Foundation, the MacDowell Colony, and Virginia Center for the Creative Arts for fellowships which gave me both the time and inspiration for many of these poems. I also wish to thank the Ludwig Vogelstein Foundation and the National Endowment for the Arts for needed grants. Also the Heart's Desire poets—Laurie Duesing, Christina Hauck, Ron Salisbury—for their lovingly rigorous criticism, and especially Dorianne Laux, sister traveler, for rowing when I couldn't.

About the Author

Kim Addonizio was born in Washington, DC, in 1954. She briefly attended Georgetown University and then studied music at American University before moving to San Francisco. She has worked as a waitress, cook, secretary, portrait photographer, tennis instructor, and attendant for the disabled. At the age of twenty-eight she completed an undergraduate degree at San Francisco State University and went to work in an auto parts store for four years while earning a Master's in Creative Writing. Since then she has taught at universities, prisons, senior centers, and hospitals. Her awards include a Fellowship from the National Endowment for the Arts. She currently teaches privately and at Vista College in Berkeley, and lives in San Francisco with her daughter, Aya.

BOA EDITIONS, LTD.

NEW POETS OF AMERICA SERIES

Vol. 1   *Cedarhome*
          Poems by Barton Sutter
          Foreword by W.D. Snodgrass

Vol. 2   *Beast Is a Wolf with Brown Fire*
          Poems by Barry Wallenstein
          Foreword by M.L. Rosenthal

Vol. 3   *Along the Dark Shore*
          Poems by Edward Byrne
          Foreword by John Ashbery

Vol. 4   *Anchor Dragging*
          Poems by Anthony Piccione
          Foreword by Archibald MacLeish

Vol. 5   *Eggs in the Lake*
          Poems by Daniela Gioseffi
          Foreword by John Logan

Vol. 6   *Moving the House*
          Poems by Ingrid Wendt
          Foreword by William Stafford

Vol. 7   *Whomp and Moonshiver*
          Poems by Thomas Whitbread
          Foreword by Richard Wilbur

Vol. 8   *Where We Live*
          Poems by Peter Makuck
          Foreword by Louis Simpson

Vol. 9   *Rose*
          Poems by Li-Young Lee
          Foreword by Gerald Stern

Vol. 10   *Genesis*
          Poems by Emanuel di Pasquale
          Foreword by X.J. Kennedy

Vol. 11   *Borders*
          Poems by Mary Crow
          Foreword by David Ignatow

Vol. 12   *Awake*
          Poems by Dorianne Laux
          Foreword by Philip Levine

Vol. 13   *Hurricane Walk*
          Poems by Diann Blakely Shoaf
          Foreword by William Matthews

Vol. 14   *The Philosopher's Club*
          Poems by Kim Addonizio
          Foreword by Gerald Stern